LEBRON JAMES
Basketball Superstar

BY JOANNE MATTERN

CAPSTONE PRESS
a capstone imprint

Sports Illustrated KIDS Superstar Athletes is published by Capstone Press,
151 Good Counsel Drive, P.O. Box 669, Mankato, Minnesota 56002.
www.capstonepub.com

Books published by Capstone Press are manufactured with paper
containing at least 10 percent post-consumer waste.

Library of Congress Cataloging-in-Publication Data
Mattern, Joanne, 1963–
   Lebron James : basketball superstar / by Joanne Mattern.
      p. cm.—(Sports illustrated kids, superstar athletes)
   Includes bibliographical references and index.
   Summary: "Presents the athletic biography of LeBron James, including his career as a high school and
professional basketball player"—Provided by publisher.
   ISBN 978-1-4296-6562-9 (library binding)
   ISBN 978-1-4296-7309-9 (paperback)
   1. James, LeBron—Juvenile literature. 2. Basketball players—United States—Biography—
Juvenile literature. 3. African American basketball players—Biography—Juvenile literature.
I. Title. II. Series.
   GV884.J36 M378 2012
   796.323092—dc22[B]   2011001024

Editorial Credits
Christopher L. Harbo, editor; Ted Williams, designer; Eric Gohl, media researcher;
    Eric Manske, production specialist

Photo Credits
AP Images/Tony Dejak, 5
Getty Images/NBAE/David Liam Kyle, 6
Newscom/Icon SMI 581/Bob Falcetti, 9
Sports Illustrated/Al Tielemans, 10, 12; Bill Frakes, 22 (middle); Bob Rosato, cover (all), 19;
    David E. Klutho, 1, 17; John Biever, 2–3, 16, 23, 24; John W. McDonough, 11, 13, 21, 22 (top &
    bottom); Manny Millan, 15

Design Elements
Shutterstock/chudo-yudo, designerpix, Fassver Anna, Fazakas Mihaly

Direct Quotations
Pages 8 from September 22, 2005, interview on *The Oprah Winfrey Show*, http://www.oprah.com
Page 20 from interview sessions held at a 2003 Chicago pre-draft camp on June 7-8,
    www.insidehoops.com

Printed in the United States of America in North Mankato, Minnesota.
032011   006110CGF11

TABLE OF CONTENTS

CHAPTER 1

HOT SHOT

On March 27, 2004, the Cleveland Cavaliers faced the New Jersey Nets. The Cavs' 19-year-old star, LeBron James, started out cold. He missed his first three shots. But by the end of the first quarter, he turned up the heat. James ended the first half with 13 points.

James' hot shooting continued in the second half. He added 12 points in the third quarter. His 16 points in the fourth quarter were capped off with a slam dunk. When the game ended, James had 41 points. He was the youngest National Basketball Association (NBA) player to score 40 points in a game.

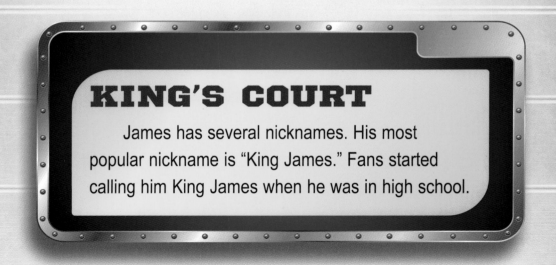

KING'S COURT

James has several nicknames. His most popular nickname is "King James." Fans started calling him King James when he was in high school.

CHAPTER 2

SIMPLE BEGINNINGS

LeBron James was born December 30, 1984, in Akron, Ohio. He and his mother, Gloria, didn't have much money. They moved often. Gloria wanted a better life for him. She sent him to live with his football coach, Frankie Walker. Walker gave the fourth-grader a good home.

"I think the reason why I'm the person who I am today is because I went through those tough times when I was younger."
—LeBron James

    James' two favorite sports were
football and basketball. By high school,
James ruled the basketball court.
In his freshman year, his team won
the state championship.

The next year, James **averaged** more than 25 points a game. He was named Ohio's top high school player. His team won its second state championship in a row.

average—to find the typical number of points scored or rebounds grabbed in each game

As a junior, James averaged 29 points a game. He was named National Player of the Year. In his senior year, James' average rose above 31

points a game. NBA **scouts** watched him win a third state championship. He was pictured on the cover of *Sports Illustrated*.

scout—someone sent to watch and assess players and teams

CHAPTER 3

KING JAMES

In 2003 the Cleveland Cavaliers
drafted James right out of high
school. In his first game, he scored
25 points. At the end of the season,
he was named **Rookie** of the Year.
By James' third season, he averaged
more than 30 points a game.

draft—to choose a person to join a sports team
rookie—a first-year player

In 2006–2007, James averaged more than 27 points and six **rebounds** a game. He also led the Cavaliers to their first NBA Finals.

rebound—the act of gaining possession of the ball after a missed shot

During 2007–2008, James couldn't
be stopped. He averaged 30 points a
game. He became the youngest player
to score 10,000 points.

James had another great season in 2008–2009. He led his team in scoring, rebounds, **assists**, steals, and blocks. The Cavaliers reached the Eastern Conference Finals. During 2009–2010, James averaged more than 27 points a game. The Cavs made the playoffs again.

assist—a pass that leads to a score by a teammate

OLYMPIC TEAMS

James has been a member of two U.S. Olympic basketball teams. In 2004 his team won the bronze medal in Athens, Greece. In 2008 his team took home the gold medal in Beijing, China.

CHAPTER 4

MIAMI HEAT

James' **contract** with the Cavaliers ended in 2010. That summer, people wondered where he would play next. Finally, James signed with the Miami Heat. Cavalier fans were upset to see their star player leave. But King James will rule the court for years to come.

contract—a legal agreement between a team and a player

"I don't need too much. Glamour and all that stuff don't excite me. I am just glad I have the game of basketball in my life."—LeBron James

TIMELINE

1984—LeBron James is born December 30 in Akron, Ohio.

2000—James leads Saint Vincent-Saint Mary High School to its second state basketball championship in a row; he is named Ohio's Mr. Basketball.

2003—James is drafted by the Cleveland Cavaliers.

2004—James is named the NBA Rookie of the Year.

2007—James leads the Cavaliers to the NBA finals.

2008—James becomes the youngest NBA player to score 10,000 career points; he wins a gold medal as part of the U.S. Olympic Basketball Team.

2010—James leaves the Cavaliers and signs with the Miami Heat.

GLOSSARY

assist (uh-SIST)—a pass that leads to a score by a teammate

average (AV-uh-rij)—to find the typical number of points scored or rebounds grabbed in each game

contract (KAHN-trakt)—a legal agreement between a team and a player

draft (DRAFT)—to choose a person to join a sports team

rebound (REE-bound)—the act of gaining possession of the ball after a missed shot

rookie (RUK-ee)—a first-year player

scout (SKOUT)—someone sent to watch and assess players and teams

READ MORE

Ladewski, Paul. *NBA: Megastars 2010.* New York: Scholastic, 2010.

Osier, Dan. *LeBron James*. Basketball's MVPs. New York: PowerKids Press, 2011.

INTERNET SITES

FactHound offers a safe, fun way to find Internet sites related to this book. All of the sites on FactHound have been researched by our staff.

Here's all you do:

Visit *www.facthound.com*

Type in this code: 9781429665629

 **Super-cool stuff!** Check out projects, games and lots more at **www.capstonekids.com**

INDEX